Building Back from Disaster

A Handbook for Leaders

Bill Nicol

For humanitarian leaders who sacrifice much in helping affected communities rebuild after a disaster

First published 2014 by NicolNotes

ISBN: 978-0-9942091-5-3 (print edition)
ISBN: 978-0-9942091-4-6 (ebook edition)

The Author

Bill Nicol is an independent advisor to government, business and the humanitarian community. Trained as a journalist, honed as an investigative author, seasoned as a management consultant and tempered as a disaster recovery leader, he works across all facets of organizational leadership, strategy and development, and tours as an international consultant, coach, speaker and trainer. With long experience in crisis response and disaster recovery, he played a pivotal role in helping lead the recovery of Aceh from the 2004 tsunami. His six-volume opus, *Tsunami Chronicles: Adventures in Disaster Management* (2013), is the definitive study of Aceh's reconstruction and a seminal work on international disaster recovery. After completing *Chronicles*, he wrote *Crisis Leadership: Dealing with Disasters from Asia to Africa and America* (2014) and *Tsunami: A Poet's Journey* (2014) before completing his trilogy for the tsunami's 10th anniversary with *Building Back from Disasters: A Handbook for Leaders* (2014). These books add to his earlier investigations in *Timor* (*Stillborn Nation* 1978, *Nation Reborn* 2002) and *McBride: Behind the Myth* (1989). You can find Bill at www.nicolnotes.com. His US agent is Vikki Wells at www.ThatAGirlSpeakers.com.

CONTENTS

CHAPTER ONE

Defining the Territory

Disasters are not nice. They arrive unexpectedly and with such force that they overwhelm our capacity to respond, at least initially. But respond we must if we are to recover. Doping so effectively requires leadership, the subject of this handbook.

Deliberately short, it offers a general set of ideas rather than proscriptions for how to respond to disasters. I have written it based on my own experience working in and writing about disaster management.

I oversaw the recovery of Aceh following the 2004 Indian Ocean Tsunami as the Indonesian Government's senior advisor and analyzed the recovery program at length in *Tsunami Chronicles*. I then wrote *Crisis Leadership* to broaden the analysis.

Friends and colleagues have encouraged me to go further by writing a disaster practitioner's manual. That would be a step too far, however, as I am no expert in all aspects of disaster recovery. I have, for instance, no medical training so could not tell you how to set up or run an emergency medical center. Neither could I tell you how to reestablish a catastrophically broken supply chain. I will leave such things to those with expertise in the relevant fields.

My knowledge and experience is far more general. It concerns the role of leadership in responding to and rebuilding from a natural disaster like an earthquake or tsunami. That is what I will concentrate on here without trying to cover every eventuality from every perspective. Even so, I will assume that the disaster involves some human catastrophe requiring a large-scale, multi-party response potentially overseen at a government or inter-governmental level; and that you have the common sense to extrapolate any principles and pointers to your own situation, role and resources. Use what makes sense, reject what does not.

While I offer an explanatory example here and there, I have kept the narrative to a minimum. If you need further clarification, please read my earlier books for the anecdotal entertainments likely to enrich your appreciation. A taste of these follows.

* * *

My first book on disasters is *Timor: The Stillborn Nation* (1978). I later updated and republished this for the independence of Timor-Leste under a new subtitle, *A Nation Reborn* (2002).

Timor is an investigation into the politics of man-made disasters. These can have a long tail, as in long-neglected East Timor that suffered for centuries beneath the stultifying hand of decaying Portuguese colonialism only to be suddenly released by a revolution in Lisbon that toppled the old colonial order.

The new politics of East Timor went through four critical internal stages: enthusiastic but naive exuberance at newfound political freedom; sharpening political divisions as new political groupings competed for popular support; embittered ideological zealotry as the battle lines hardened; civil war as the political combatants turned into military ones.

Running parallel with these went two external forces. One was the ungraceful rush of the Portuguese colonial administrators to exit East Timor as fast as they could, happily allowing the local political infighting to boil over into open warfare as an excuse for exiting with undue haste. The other was the Indonesian military behemoth unwilling to allow the emergence on its doorstep of any fractious, left-leaning country that might encourage deeper divisions in its own centrifugal polity. The result was an Indonesian invasion and quarter-century occupation before East Timor finally achieved its independence.

The whole thing was an avoidable man-made disaster where tens of thousands lost this lives. Better, more determined Portuguese leadership may well have prevented the catastrophe, as may a more open and less-militarized Indonesia, a more sophisticated and supportive contribution by East Timor's regional neighbors and a more adroit and cautious local political leadership within East Timor itself.

But, of course, it was not to be. Few cared about East Timor as it languished beneath the Portuguese yoke over several centuries. The region happily accepted the status quo while everything remained quiet and docile. So there was little if any preparation. All the parties were caught off guard by the unexpected revolution in Lisbon. Policy failures followed as the main players suddenly woke up to trouble on their doorstep. In place of gradual transition supported by a constructive political, economic and social development program, the politics of East Timor ran out of control by erupting into full blown war and military occupation with all the nasty consequences.

My next book, *McBride: Behind the Myth* (1989), explored a different sort of disaster. It too was man-made and, therefore, entirely avoidable. But this time reputations were lost instead of lives.

At its heart, *McBride* examines how one man rose to international fame only to fall from grace and see his private research institute collapse when he was discovered to have committed scientific fraud. While the book looks at the house of cards on which this fame was built, it is far more than a book about an individual whose life ran off the rails. Rather, it concerns the deeper issues of how we govern ourselves as a society, how the leadership and governance of organizations can fail, how good people in responsible positions turn a blind eye to failings they forgive out of good but misguided intent, the role of the media in lazily accepting and reinforcing a false public image and the blindness of a community that creates and leans on supposed heroes to simplify the complexities of life.

I could go on but you hopefully get the picture. *McBride* may revolve around an individual but is fundamentally concerned with a corporate disaster that had been waiting in the wings fed by a publicity machine that built the McBride myth to such heights there was only one way it could go when the balloon burst—down, fast and hard! The resulting crisis and consequent disaster could have been avoided if people in responsible positions had done their job properly, a common story in the world of corporate disasters when many can see them coming but do nothing or are blocked from doing something to prevent them.

There was a long pause between writing *McBride* and my next book, *Tsunami Chronicles: Adventures in Disaster Management* (2013), during which I spent years building a consulting practice helping clients prepare for and respond to various crises and disasters. This experience culminated in a request to help the Indonesian Government plan its response to the 2004 Indian Ocean Tsunami and then become its senior advisor for tsunami recovery in Aceh. The four years I then spent in the belly of Indonesia's tsunami recovery, observing and participating in its many dimensions within Indonesia and across the world sharpened my appreciation of disaster leadership at a global level.

Ultimately, the experience reinforced my view that the success of any disaster response hinges on the quality of those selected to lead the response. Good leaders prevent and resolve crises, bad ones create them. I saw this within Indonesia's purpose-built tsunami reconstruction agency, BRR, and across the length and breadth of the international players who contributed. Ideological narrowness, political nastiness, organizational atrophy, individual selfishness and collective sourness all contributed to the mix of disablers that daily sought to derail recovery operations. Only through consistently good and determined leadership did we defeat them.

Despite this, sour politics can still defeat the best of leaders, particularly when the wrong lessons are transported from one disaster to another, as they were from Aceh to Haiti, only to cause more problems. Preventing this requires vigilance. Disaster leaders need to be alert to the political games that can cripple any crisis response because they can only manage what they know or can see. If blind to them, the leaders will struggle and probably be defeated.

Disasters offer an imperfect landscape for leaders. While all disasters may look the same on the surface, they will be different beneath. It is why no handbook like his can provide leaders with a script for every eventuality. Even so, we can draw out the common elements, as I did in my most recent book, *Crisis Leadership: Dealing with Disasters from Asia to Africa and America* (2014).

This plucks the most common features from a rich field of crisis leadership to confront the leadership and organizational failures that give rise to or block effective responses. The World Bank and World Health Organization come in for special mention, although I arrive at a despondent conclusion with regard to them—namely that their very structures and cultures ultimately doom them to fail as crisis leaders.

I take WHO's laggardly response to the outbreak of Ebola in West Africa as one typical case, the World Bank's internal gyrations in relation to Aceh as another. Large, global entities like WHO are geared contractually, financially and organizationally to deliver ongoing programs instead of responding to crises; and, most disheartening of all, there is little they can do about this because, inevitably, the corporate demands for order and control ultimately outweigh and outplay the need for urgency, speed and adaptability any crisis demands. The Bank escaped the noose of bureaucratic inertia in the early part of the Aceh program only to be ensnared by it later.

The demoralizing feature of this is that while such problems are predictable they may not be preventable. The bureaucratic culture of any organization can work in "normal" times only to entirely fail when confronted with anything out of the ordinary, particularly a disaster. The unexpected can leave those at the top floundering; and, even if they initially cope, the organizational cultures over which they preside can return with a vengeance before the crisis has passed to cripple the urgency and initiative required to confront it.

* * *

When disasters strike, the challenges are many. We'll come to some of the main ones in the following chapter. Before we get there, a word about assumptions, two in particular.

Every disaster plan is built on a set of assumptions which may or may not be properly articulated or even valid. One is that disasters only happen to others, not ourselves; that we are immune to them. This leads to complacency where those in responsible positions disregard any serious preparations.

The other is that whatever preparations they may have or put in place will actually work if or when a disaster strikes. I observed this with the tsunami in Indonesia and Typhoon Haiyan in the Philippines. Both countries had established disaster management systems that proved totally inadequate to the disasters they confronted.

Indonesia responded best of the two not because of the established response capacities but because it had a fresh new team of national leaders able and willing to respond creatively by establishing a new agency under a new minister with bold new powers. The Philippines looked sludgy, slow and tired in comparison, its entrenched politics inadequate to the task. The quality of national leadership in both cases again proved the defining element in the two responses.

The only safe assumption is that a disaster of some sort is heading your way right now so you better be ready for it. The last thing you want is to look like then president René Préval stumbling forlornly through the crumbled ruins of Port-o-

Prince after Haiti's 2010 earthquake clueless about what to do.

I suspect Préval's problem lay in confusing a technical response from one of leadership. Technically, there can be no doubt that the immensity of Haiti's earthquake totally overwhelmed the limited capacity of its inadequate government to respond in any meaningful way. But there is always something a leader can do, not least use the media to reflect the pain of the affected community while calling on the international community to come and help.

That, in part, is what this book concerns itself with. It is not just that leaders *can* do something but that they *must*. Affected communities look to leaders for hope, confidence and meaning, emotional touchstones that have less to do with any technical response and more with the fact that, no matter how limited the technical capacities may be, at least there is someone taking the lead to do something to do something meaningful in response.

* * *

Disaster leadership is an extension of crisis leadership which, in turn, is an extension of leadership more generally. It requires a sharper focus on the fundamental elements of leadership within a dramatically demanding context. As a leader's handbook, *Building Back from Disasters* attempts to provide this focus while also wrapping the subject in the more ordinary clothes of universal leadership. You will therefore find within it some very general along with some more specific material.

Given this, let's put a definitional handle on the subject. While I use dictionaries extensively, I also like to give things intellectual shape by defining terms in my own way. This is an important skill for leaders as they must first shape things intellectually if they are then to produce practical results.

Hence the following definitions. You'll find them running through each of my previous leadership books in some way, most specifically in *Crisis Leadership*. They're not perfect. But they do capture the essence of how I view the subject...

Crisis—a time of intense difficulty, trouble or danger involving grave risk if not addressed with resolute urgency

Disaster—a tragedy that overtakes the ability of individuals, communities or even nations to respond or recover without external help

Leadership—the independent exercise of personal initiative often, but not necessarily, to leverage cooperative contributions to achieve an objective

Crisis Leadership—the exercise of determined technical, personal or political skills and authority to establish, deploy and leverage resources in containing, mitigating and recovering from a crisis or disaster

You'll notice here I've skipped a specific definition of disaster leadership. Instead, I've included it within the notion of crisis leadership because any disaster creates a crisis. Yet disaster leadership demands something more if only because a disaster involves quantum leap beyond what may generally be regarded as a crisis.

In the context of a human catastrophe like an earthquake, tsunami, fire, flood, landslide, typhoon, tornado or volcanic eruption that kills, injures, maims and destroys just about everything in its vicinity, a disaster demands an immediate humanitarian response to save lives, provide food and shelter, restore livelihoods and rebuild infrastructure. This can be an immense undertaking, particularly if the scale is large, the spread of damage is wide, the location is remote, the supply chain is broken and the established response mechanisms completely outmatched and overwhelmed. Add a war to the equation and things get even more difficult.

In such circumstances, the whole concept of leadership takes on a new meaning. For a disaster invalidates all previous assumptions. Any who respond must begin from scratch. I have thought about this at length in developing the following definition. It includes but extends the concept of crisis leadership.

Disaster Leadership—stepping out in front in a moment of great tragedy and destruction to take charge of rebuilding communities and infrastructure shattered by man or nature

This draws on my Aceh experience. I could have added something about the *how*, like rebuilding through a coordinated emergency response that delivers the best results in the shortest time with the least harm using available resources, but that would detract from the main point. Disasters involve destruction. Disaster leadership is concerned with rebuilding.

Disaster leaders will face many challenges in doing this, the subject of the next chapter.

CHAPTER TWO

What to Expect

What can you expect if you take on the job of leading a disaster recovery program? Just about everything from good to bad and in between. The obstacles will be endless. The potholes will be deep. The pitfalls will take your breath away. Murphy's law will prevail to the power of ten. Whatever can go wrong will go wrong and at the worst possible moment in the worst possible way. Just as you think things are going well, the world will probably fall apart around you. But it won't be all doom and gloom. There will be some sunny days, special moments when you take heart that the job you are doing is going okay and very worthwhile.

Problems come with the job of disaster leadership. Expect them and you won't be disappointed, anticipate them and you won't be caught by surprise, prepare for them and you might even turn them to advantage. Just don't give up. No matter how dark the day, something good will ultimately come from it if you persist.

That is why I have written this chapter. I want to give you a sense of what might be coming your way as you step into role as a disaster leader. I've written the chapter assuming you will be working right on location in a disaster far from home base. If you are one of the early responders, expect to be overwhelmed by what you find amid the overwhelming chaos, suffering and despair. There will be too much for anyone to do. As a leader, your job is not to rush in but to step back from the detail to assess how the skills and resources you bring can make the greatest difference in the shortest time.

Things are likely to become clearer over time as you gradually organize and deploy your resources to do what you can as you can. But you will still be overwhelmed by the magnitude of the task. There will never be enough hours in the day to do everything. One problem will overtake another in rapid succession. Exhaustion will lay its hands on you and your team as everyone is stretched to their limits. Goodwill will be sorely tested.

And that is just for starters. Far more difficult problems are likely to await you, some from the most unexpected quarters. Take that insidious beast we call office politics, the elephant in the room that is ever ready to squash you.

Head Office Politics

Hypothetically, you probably got loads of support from colleagues in head office when you accepted the job. They patted you on the back and wished you well as you departed. But that was a while ago. Over time, the mood has changed.

The managers in head office now can't understand why you are not moving faster and are disappointed with the quality of your reports. They keep demanding more and more reports to justify expenses and satisfy information requests from those further up the chain of command.

Tensions mount as your own requests for more resources seem to fall on deaf ears and head office reporting demands conflict with your wider leadership responsibilities. Misunderstandings abound and trust fails as each side comes to see the other as incompetent, abrasive and obstructive. A power clash is inevitable as personal animosities sharpen.

There is little you can do about this while stationed out in the field as a disaster leader. You have many other overriding priorities to deal with so just put up with problems hoping head office will wake up to itself and the problems will go away. But it doesn't and they won't.

The picture from head office is far different. There, the senior managers seethe with anger at what they regard as your contempt for their authority. Their ego is on the line along with their status as disaster champions. They will allow nothing to threaten these.

Like you, the head office managers are busy people. After all, they have their meetings to attend and in-trays to clear. Feeding the internal machinery of bureaucratic necessity takes time. It is the way of things. Those at the center can rarely see the cultural inertia that holds them in its grip. Power is theirs. Everything else is peripheral to it. The intensity of this may vary from time to time but remains fairly constant.

Head office hierarchical arrangements reinforce this. The head honchos sit at the top of the power pyramid with everyone else below. The pecking order is clearly defined by rank. This continues down the line in the chicken-factory of bureaucracy. Peckees quickly become peckers.

Those deployed to the field to lead or work in a humanitarian disaster in some distant corner of the world are vulnerable to the consequences. Out of the political loop, they are expected to either genuflect to senior managers in head office or pay the price if they don't.

I have seen and experienced the problem first hand. It's a classic, it's ugly and it happens. People working in the field get undermined, attacked and sacked with little or no chance to defend themselves.

Need it be like this? No. It can be reversed by a willful inversion of the hierarchical model where head office serves the field instead of the other way around. Just don't hold your breath waiting for this to happen; and, if it does, don't expect the honeymoon to last.

Media Madness

One way to protect yourself from head office politics is to develop an independent profile of yourself as an indispensable disaster leader. Here, the media can be your greatest asset. Disasters are good news for journalists. Human interest is their stock in trade and where there is suffering there is interest.

As a disaster leader, expect visiting journalists to land on your doorstep looking for a story. Feed them as much as you can. As the person out front, it's your job to represent and promote your program interests so make time to educate and help reporters no matter how much of a distraction they may seem. The media can help you put the spotlight on the human dimensions of the disaster as well as the difficulties you are facing in a way that nothing else can. Financial, political and organizational support can follow.

But take care. While most reporting is likely to be sympathetic to anyone helping disaster-affected communities, some reporting can be a death blow. Ignorant journalists clueless of the problems and demands of disaster leadership but keen on a headline can write highly damaging reports. Again, I have experienced this first hand. There's not a lot you can do in response and don't expect anyone to jump to your defense if it happens.

Even so, most negative media reports are likely to be critical of government rather than humanitarian leaders and any criticism is likely be along the line that things are "going too slow" due to a lack of resources and support rather than poor leadership. This bad news can be good news for you, so be ready to highlight problems but take care in who or what you blame. The backwash can be intense.

Be especially careful of visiting celebrities who come with a media entourage. They can be well meaning as well as dangerously self-serving. While celebrity attention can be a force multiplier in gaining public and political support, it can also distort program priorities if misdirected.

Difficult People

Disasters attract the best and worst of people because of the large sums of money often involved. Connivers, corruptors and carpet baggers come out of the woodwork in droves pushing all sorts of things, some useful, others not. So keep your wits about you.

Some of the most difficult are VIPs from the big agencies who come bearing gifts of big bucks. Some, perhaps most, are highly professional and a delight to work with. Others can be pompous idiots who, thinking they know better than anyone else, throw their weight around like a bull in the china shop hardly noticing the damage they cause. Don't expect the most ethical behaviours from them either. Process abuse can be their stock in trade as they play hard ball projecting and protecting their interests.

Still, these people at least bring money to the table so are an asset to be tapped if you can. A little shmoozing can go a long way. On the other hand, be careful of disaster tourists looking for an easy ride on the backs of others. Plenty of lazy incompetents turn up in disasters, people who can't get a job elsewhere. Weed them out as fast as you can.

Disaster victims can also be difficult to work with. It will likely be a mixed lot. Some will be grateful for any help you give. Others, hopefully very few, will resent your intrusions, particularly if you upset their entrenched interests. Some will actively help their communities. Others will greedily look after themselves. Some will help maintain calm and order. Others will rabble rouse. Some will look after you to their last breath. Others will threaten and extort.

I could go on with more in this vein but it's all much of a muchness when you unpack it. People are people. Some are good, some bad. Some are constructive, some destructive. Some make a positive contribution, some block and undermine. The job of leadership is to judge people on their merits and use or discard them accordingly.

Disaster Dynamics

Disasters are rarely static. Their mood and dynamic changes over time, as do associated attitudes. People who once supported you can turn against you just as former foes can become firm friends. You can be left lonely and alone when people you worked alongside intensively over a long period pack their bags to go home at the end of their posting.

As a disaster leader, you will need to cope with and adapt to these developments if you stay the course. You will also need to exercise care in the dynamics your own program initiatives create or contribute to. Good intentions can lead to difficult outcomes. In Haiti, shanty towns rose where food was distributed following the 2010 earthquake limiting reconstruction options in the land-strapped capital of Port-au-Prince.

Such things happen in the urgency of disaster response. Saving lives takes precedence over the more complex area of land planning. Recovery programs have to adapt as best they can. Disaster leaders must be on their toes in doing so while appreciating both current recovery dynamics and their possible progression.

To help in this, here are some of the progressions I observed in Aceh's recovery from the 2004 tsunami. While not suggesting all recovery programs will be the same, the following are indicative of what you might expect as a disaster leader. You can read the longer version in *Tsunami Chronicles*.

In theory, there are four stages in disaster recovery:

1. *Emergency response*—helping survivors with immediate needs for food, water, shelter and medical assistance
2. *Rehabilitation*—clearing debris and returning lightly damaged but usable infrastructure to working order
3. *Reconstruction*—the serious job rebuilding communities, economies and infrastructure

4. *Development*—the longer-term process of strengthening the economic, social and political foundations of a community

Looking at things from within the government reconstruction agency to which I was attached in Indonesia, I saw a different progression. Marked in years, it went something like this:

1. Building the operational base and core recovery momentum while fighting for political space as a coordinating agency
2. Settling into the reconstruction rhythm while riven by internal politics that effectively split the agency in two
3. Managing confrontations with local communities and the rising contempt by some international partners
4. Tidying up loose ends while turning inward to celebrate success in the grip of victory disease

As for the affected communities, they too went through a progression all their own. It evolved like this:

1. *Disabling shock* as communities were smashed by the earthquake and tsunami
2. *Relief* as communities gained sense of hope as aid flowed in
3. *Gratitude* as cash-for-work and livelihood programs kicked in
4. *Dependency* as recipients became hooked on the largesse of donors
5. *Greed* as people exploited opportunities to get more than their share
6. *Rage* at perceived recovery failures as opportunities to exploit donor aid came to an end

End Games

As the evolving dynamics suggest, things can get worse rather than better over the course of a disaster recovery program. Helping those in need can prove counter-productive by creating destructive attitudes and dependencies. Even disaster leaders can find their attitudes souring as they gloat over their perceived success in the distortional grip of personal exhaustion.

No less a problem lies in the so-called lessons that are publicly documented during or at the end of a disaster recovery program. It's rare to find any that are genuine let alone honest. Serious problems are whitewashed, mistakes ignored, contributions exaggerated and managerial ignorance perpetuated.

Yet some lessons are taken to heart, particularly the political ones, although are not always helpful. Haiti got the wrong end of the pineapple in the political lessons the European Commission transferred from its experience in Aceh to infect Haiti's earthquake recovery. These compromised the governing architecture of Haiti's recovery thereby damaging recovery efforts right from the start.

Since the end of one recovery program forms a base for the next, disaster leaders need to consider the published lessons with care, and, in most cases, probably take them with a grain of salt.

CHAPTER THREE

Recovery Architecture

The governing architecture of a disaster recovery program can make or break it. It deserves special attention.

This chapter is for those responsible—governments. They have a special role in establishing the frameworks for and leading a disaster response. That, after all, is one of the reasons we create them: to provide local and national leadership in good times and bad.

In responding to a disaster, governments have four broad options:

1. Work through established local and national agencies, preferably by nominating one as the lead agency
2. Create a new, purpose-built agency to lead recovery operations
3. Appoint an individual with overarching authority to coordinate the efforts of all the government agencies without creating any new ones
4. Rely on an external body like the United Nations to oversee and coordinate recovery operations

Which is best? That depends on the circumstances. If established structures work well and can respond with the required speed and efficacy, there's no need for any new ones. If not, something new will be needed. In the case of a country entirely dependent on a body like the UN, it still needs to establish some political oversight and guidance.

On the assumption that a government wants to help an affected community, questionable in some cases, any structure it adopts will still need leadership by an individual with authority and single-point accountability to drive recovery forward. There can be a lot of pushing and shoving over this as the politics of power play out, but, ultimately, a leader without the strongest political mandate and legal authority will be a lame duck.

Be of a mind to negotiate hard if your government ever chooses you to head such an operation. You will either win or lose the end game depending on the power you get at the front end. Pay attention to the fine print. You may be given some general authority only to find yourself toothless without the corresponding implementing regulations. Likewise, you'll need to get your hands on the money. Regardless of your political power, your financial power will likewise dictate success or failure. You must get the money directly under your control. Your power will be dramatically weakened if it flows through other agencies instead of your own.

Assuming you have both political, legal and financial power, your next step will be to gain administrative power by bringing within your agency or office any government functions that have a role in or impact on your operations. Aim to make it a one-stop administrative shop where all permits, visas, security, tax and other matters can be approved or settled in one place. This is particularly helpful in a corrupt environment where individual officials in other agencies can use their positions to delay approvals until a bribe is paid. Bringing in delegates from other agencies with the required processing authorities makes the process far more transparent and controllable. It also makes it faster.

Handling money is the one exception to this. Given the cumbersome nature of government finances, you are probably better off having control of the money but no responsibility for handling it. Managing money is a treasury function better kept at arms length. Securing, disbursing, counting, reporting on and accounting for money is a specialized business. It can consume a lot of resources and be a significant distraction from core recovery business. Just ensure that any treasury functions serving you are dedicated to the task so they are fully responsive. This will show in the speed with which contractor invoices are paid.

In a disaster, cash is king. It is the one of the greatest enablers. The quicker it flows the quicker recovery will progress. Money for food. Cash for work. Fast-track procurement. All have their place in rebuilding communities after a disaster. As will corruption, which you should fight from the start through a dedicated anti-corruption function that treats corruption as a core strategic threat. Your program and reputation depend on it.

There are two other strategic functions you must attend to. You should appoint a Chief of Staff to take a broad view over general strategy, operating architecture, stakeholder relations and politics and a Chief of Operations to oversee everything of a technical nature from engineering designs to project approvals, information management to logistics.

Together, the support of these two roles free you to be what you need to be, the overall disaster leader.

As for the operations themselves, place these as close to the disaster area as possible, preferably right on the spot. It's the only way to be on top of and responsive to recovery needs and fast-paced developments. If the disaster is spread over a wide area, you'll also need a regional structure but, paradoxically, while this will keep you close to the action it will also be more difficult to control and protect. Security may become an issue as dispersed offices are more vulnerable to political and criminal attacks from affected communities than a central one.

If there are loads of delivery partners you may need to create additional coordinating structures to direct and support them. That's what we did in Aceh by creating a dedicated UN Office Recovery Coordinator (UNORC). It operated by government mandate but was independent of the government and acted as an operational interface between the government reconstruction agency and the field operations of our largest partners, including 27 UN agencies, funds and programs. UNORC in turn managed the Interagency Standing Committee, an established UN coordinating mechanism for the larger contributors. It was far easier to look after these at arms length through an independent mechanism than to do so ourselves although we also worked with each partner independently.

Delivery partners can and will also create their own coordinating structures either between themselves or in specific clusters that bring together organizations with particular interests or common capacities. It is easier to leave partners to lead and coordinate these efforts among themselves than to do it yourself although it makes sense to have your own specialist people participate in the groups.

One group it is essential that you do form, lead and coordinate is that for project approvals. This gives you at least a semblance of control over what projects are delivering what and where. It also helps to identify gaps, readjust imbalances and respond to emerging priorities. Flexibility in the approval process is essential as it takes time to work out where reconstruction resources should be directed; and partners often need a little pushing and shoving so they don't concentrate on the most accessible areas where they can get the highest profile.

Your own agency will likewise need resource flexibility for the same reasons. You will maximise this by having a one-line appropriation that allows you to allocate your own resources where and when you see fit. Beware any well-intentioned but highly detailed project lists imposed on you by other government agencies. They might tick a box for thoroughness but, if you are bound by them, also leave you unable to adapt to changing needs and circumstances, particularly if each item is allocated its own budget you must deliver and report against. It is better to start with a more general, back-of-envelope plan that allows plenty of room to adapt than a highly detailed one that does not. The same goes for the budget cycle. You are better off working from a flexible trust fund where money can be rolled from year to year to avoid the constipation of an annual budget cycle that is completely out of place in any emergency recovery operation.

As for how you spend your money, this can be tricky. If you have plenty of delivery partners and your primary job is to coordinate their activities, do not run your own construction operations. Outsource them instead by funding delivery partners with proven and scalable capacities. If you do otherwise by implementing your own programs, you risk competing head-on with delivery partners instead of coordinating and supporting them. Good intentions can pave the way to hell if this happens.

The same applies to coordination more generally. Do not confuse coordination with communication. While the two have much in common, you should not see one as replacing the other. Both are important in their own right and require their own internal coordination. But, of the two, you will gain most benefits from coordination. It is cumbersome, time consuming, resource intensive and difficult. It is also the way to get the most from your delivery partners. See them as customers in need of a service only a government can provide. Deliver this service to the highest standards possible. By solving your partner's problems you will also prevent or solve your own.

This, of course, is easier said than done. It involves a fine balancing act between the government as regulator and the government as supporter. How you manage this will depend on the service culture you create and the manner in which you support it. Be vigilant here. The inbred tendency of governments, indeed for all bureaucracies, to regulate and control can override all other considerations thereby undermining coordination efforts unless your service leadership is strong and sustained.

Your objective should be to *enable* constructive partner contributions. It should not be to disable them, although disabling disruptive rogue elements should certainly fall within your purview.

This concept of enabling is central to how your recovery architecture should be designed and run. You should embed it in your operating culture while ensuring your own enabling structures, systems and capacities are also strong and robust. In doing so, balance the strategic and technical elements. Technical specialists lacking a strategic appreciation can get things out of whack no less than strategic generalists with no clue of specialized technical requirements.

CHAPTER FOUR

The Model (Disaster) Leader

Setting aside the role of government in leading a disaster response, let's step back to build a general model of disaster leadership. I offer it as something leaders may care to borrow from, build on or discard.

Leadership is never easy, least of all in responding to a disaster. Neither is it a popularity contest other than for professional politicians. It can be lonely and dangerous. Leaders get used, attacked, criticized, even vilified. Everything they do and say, even what they don't do and say, will be noted, scrutinized, discussed and criticized; and the choices they make will often place them in a precarious position.

While they need to keep up a positive front, for instance, they must also be on their guard against gilding the lily or unduly dismissing problems. Followers like to know that their leaders understand the problems they face and are prepared to address them directly. Articulating bad news in this context, can be good news in the minds of others by signaling a leader's recognition of substance over spin.

Leaders can't hide from this. To be effective, they cannot be invisible. Exactly the opposite. They must lead from the front, exuding caring confidence while providing a model of common endeavor others can admire and emulate.

How leaders stand up to the pressures they face is a test of character and moral fortitude. Doing the right thing is rarely easy, doing the right thing right even harder. Even so, moral courage lies at the heart of leadership, at least of good leadership.

Before we come to that, however, a few words first about the other side of things, poor leadership.

Things to Avoid

Bad leaders can be relatively easy to spot. They tend to be insular rather than expansive, mean minded rather than generous, pompous rather than principled. You can see this in their body language and manner. Working at a technical level, they are likely to see things in terms of order and control rather than the far messier stuff of entrepreneurial experiment and engagement. They also get trapped in detail, losing sight of the larger picture.

Complacency is the killer. Even the best leaders can succumb to it, particularly if exhaustion gains the upper hand. First sign of this comes when leaders lose the desire or ability for self-criticism. They see fault in others instead of themselves. The blame game follows.

The strongest of leaders can succumb to this. Indeed, their very strength can be their Achilles heel as their determination to achieve specific goals so narrows their focus that they lose sight of the wider context.

When this happens, they risk creating a political vacuum that draws in the dark forces of dysfunctional human behaviour. These contemptuously push aside the good oil of human relations—politeness, helpfulness and basic decency—as bullying, back stabbing, name calling and passive aggression push their way center stage.

Constraining these forces requires tenacity, grit, determination, courage, stamina and a thick skin. Leaders must fortify themselves within. Strong leaders do this by arming themselves with a guiding set of principles that form their personal policy framework for action. Which brings us to a positive model of leadership.

Pragmatic Principles

I cannot tell say what your guiding principles should be but can offer the following set to prompt you in developing your own. They come from observing my minister, Dr Kuntoro Mangkusubroto, in Aceh. I recorded them in *Tsunami Chronicles.* although do not necessarily endorse all and would disavow some. Soft in part, hard in others, imperfect in general, they are nonetheless as good as any you might look for in a disaster leader.

- *Believe in yourself.* Aspire to high ideals. Have fun. Hang loose. Stay flexible. Keep people guessing. Pursue reform because it is more interesting than the status quo. Improve what you can. Maintain the core while pushing the boundaries. Fight corruption. Promote integrity through accountability.
- *Work from a position of strength.* Negotiate hard before you step into a process. Stand firm on flagship issues. Stay tough until you get what you want. Get the

highest level of political authority, access and control. Minimize constraints and controls (schedules, plans, boards). Leverage supporting mechanisms.

- *Watch the politics.* Know the plot. Stay alert. Be flexible. Keep your eye on the big picture. Adapt to the environment. Manage the politics so they don't manage you. Be prudent in not directly challenging the practices of those whose power you depend on. Play others as they play you, only better. Avoid political impasse by moving forward on practical matters with tangible results.

- *Be pragmatic and practical.* Do not be blinded by ideology or any fixed or narrow mindset. Recognize that perfection is elusive and there is more than one way to skin a cat. Take the path of least resistance in solving problems. Prefer the concrete over the philosophical, the practical over the theoretical, the technical over the political, the simple over the complex, the small over the large, the informal over the formal. Focus on fundamentals. Deal with the detail but don't get trapped in it. Adjust to circumstances. Fix problems as they emerge. Keep working the basics. Do what you can do; don't worry about what you can't. Make the occasional sacrifice, even if distasteful, as the price for getting the best you can in any difficult circumstance. Survive to fight another day.

- *Exercise authority.* Let people know who is boss through bold decisions others must obey, not egotistical pomp. Be decisive whether you are right or wrong. Move things in parallel. Give subordinates the freedom to undertake assigned tasks how they like but control them through concrete task assignments with specific deadlines and quantifiable targets. Check progress regularly. Set new deadlines in the face of slippage. Solve problems by intervening directly at any level with no concern for the chain of command.

- *Manage relationships with a hard nose but soft face.* Be open to all but limit the ability of others to interfere. Tolerate technical not political failure. Demand loyalty but give only conditional loyalty in return. When pushed into a corner, prefer loyal incompetence to challenging competence. Avoid direct confrontation where you can; fight only where you must. Defer to those you depend on. Discard those you do not. Rationalize associated dissonance; it is not your fault. When bringing down the political axe choose your timing and do not signal your punches.

Dr Kuntoro applied these principles in an intuitive six-step process:

- *Understand the beast*—define the overall task, the political dynamics and operational parameters; then...
- *Get the power*—secure the political and financial resources, establish technical capacity and lean on the legitimacy of others until you establish your own; then...
- *Shape the game*—engage and manage the players, draw in potential opponents, start loosely but increase control over time, shake up structures to let people know who is in control, protect your turf; then...

- *Focus on performance*—watch the numbers, clear obstacles, solve problems, kick the occasional head to keep people on their toes; but at the same time…
- *Keep things stable*—engage assets, disengage liabilities, promote confidence, change only what you must if you must when you must; and finally…
- *Close out the game*—finish what you can, hand over what you can't, block rearguard enemy attacks, promote success and move on.

General Principles

Of course, there are many other elements of leadership beside these, more general principles if you like. When it comes to their team, for instance, good leaders actively promote good teamwork instead of taking it for granted. How? By understanding the need of people to be involved, protected and gain meaning from what they do. To this end, good leaders are facilitators rather than dictators, at least as and when the different styles are appropriate. Their highest art form is to lead constructive meetings that generate shared understanding and commitment among team members. As they do, good leaders also

- *Lead by example*—doing as they expect others to do
- *Act decisively*—applying pragmatic criteria to quickly solve everyday problems so they don't escalate
- *Seek practical solutions*—taking time out to observe, think, plan, organize and delegate
- *Show respect*—appreciating and relating to people while remembering that much of what they achieve

depends less on the quality of their delegations than the quality of the people to whom they delegate

- *Exercise power with sensitivity*—winning the respect of stakeholders with the judicious exercise of authority based on clear rules of engagement
- *Push boundaries*—questioning and challenging accepted practices
- *Create momentum*—intervening through direct action to keep things moving forward
- *Shape the future*—doing more than just rebuilding after a disaster by reforming, improving and strengthening what they can where they can
- *Temper expectations*—being neither precious nor pedantic in the fog of disasters by appreciating little will be clear and much uncertain until substantial progress is achieved

Communicating

Since leaders are the focal point of communications, they also need to consider the what, how and why of things they do and say. As a disaster leader, think of communications as a political enabler as well as a way of connecting. Stick to the bigger picture as much as possible. Avoid too much detail beyond what is required to add substance to your comments as you

- *Prepare to be visible*—give speeches and interviews, visit crisis areas, engage with contributors
- *Communicate constructively*—recognise the challenges, exude and promote confidence in overcoming them but keep expectations low

- *Communicate directly*—adopt a relaxed and informal style to engage with people at all levels
- *Shape the narrative*—explain the context, progress, challenges, needs and assumptions understanding that what you take for granted may be new to others
- *Keep people informed*—let people know of likely disappointments and disruptions in advance so they expect and are prepared for them
- *Provide reassurance* while reflecting the wide emotions of affected communities
- *Demonstrate commitment and determination* to stay the course and overcome obstacles
- *Promote others, not yourself*—show humility, diminish the importance of your own contribution while basking in the reflected glory of the recognition you give others
- *Recognise that mistakes are inevitable* as instant decisions are demanded based on limited, blurry and often contradictory information; acknowledge and apologise when things go wrong, as they will, while explaining what you will do to fix the problem

Social Media

While speaking of communication, one cannot avoid the subject of social media as this have evolved into a powerful system of information sharing and coordination.

There is no doubt that mobile computing and social media can be tremendously useful in a fast-moving disaster context assuming local telecommunication systems are up and running. They allow disaster leaders to stay with the action and on top of developments while also reporting on them. Doing so is akin to being your own journalist in real time.

This can be powerful stuff but comes at the price of adding another task, another distraction, to a role already overloaded by tremendous pressures. Still, there's always time to write some social comment somewhere, sometime even if it's just sitting on the loo (assuming you are not distracted by dysentery or some other ailment, not uncommon in disaster environments where hygiene is less than it could be).

If you are to use social media, negotiate prior publishing approvals as part of your assignment. And get all the technical stuff in place to before your workload explodes—things like a disaster blog, website, Twitter and Facebook accounts if you think they may be helpful. Once you start publishing, keep it up as best you can. Don't get carried away. Keep your posts short, simple, to the point; time and date them; and do regular checks for feedback and posts by other delivery partners if you can. But, while considering any of this, HEED THIS WARNING…

Engaging in social media, exchanging emails and so on can be no less a disaster for you and your team than the surrounding physical and humanitarian disaster you are responding to. They can generate a tremendous amount of noise and suck you dry of time, energy and enthusiasm. The infection can be pervasive. The people you are working with can become so engulfed in social communications that they have little time for anything else, particularly if they are of the more youthful generation.

I switched off my emails working on Aceh's recovery when I realised this. I saw the young people around me generating them by the thousands believing they were actually productive when they were not. Emails sent to long lists of people who then hit the "reply to all" button even just to acknowledge receipt produced a massive volume of empty, vacant but extremely noisy nothingness. I replaced this with a request for anyone who wanted to get in touch with me to send me an SMS, a very short one (pardon another tautology) at that. This dramatically reduced the volume of communications I had to deal with, cut straight to the important stuff without needing to sort through the trivia and saved me an enormous amount of time, effort and frustration. Unplugged from emails, I found face-to-face meetings far more productive even if they did seem slower or take longer to organize and attend.

Reporting

Looking at social media from a different perspective, there are some mighty management advantages worthy of serious consideration.

Take any formal reporting requirements to any distant head office you may have. These can suck up an awful lot of time and be a tremendous burden at the end of a day, week, month or whatever the agreed reporting cycle is. And by the time you get around to it you may well have forgotten what you've actually been doing because every moment passes in such an intense blur of activity.

It's easier if you have a private assistant to help document and record things, look after the day-to-day administration and so on; and you may well be able to appoint someone to this role at some point if resources allow. In the meantime and even if the resources are available and some form of electronic communication is possible to begin with, at least consider using a platform like Twitter to dash out updates on progress, developments and issues. It's a lot easier and quicker to write short, snappy tweets on the go than traditional reports; and attaching a relevant picture can easily save more than a thousand words.

Urgency

Still on the subject of communication, one thing disaster leaders must create and communicate is a sense—or, better, a state—of urgency. This sounds easy but is not.

Urgency is one of the hardest things to understand and sustain in a disaster. People get tired of constant demands to act quickly, especially those in back offices far from the main action. Their resentment at the never-ending pressure to deliver with immediacy can result in a dismissive attitude where things are deliberately slowed instead of sped up.

Speed itself can also be counter-productive as people rush into things only to make a mess of them, clog overloaded supply channels and cause chaos at distribution points lacking sufficient storage and distribution capacities. But speed is nonetheless essential. It saves lives, feeds hope and promotes order by reducing panic among affected communities. And it hinges not so much on urgency as on a culture of urgency.

What's the difference? Urgency can be short-lived, a quick flurry of activity to meet some immediate priority. But in a disaster everything is a priority, so urgency itself can become just a messy way of rushing from one thing to another in ill-considered haste. A culture of urgency is different. It is a sustained state of systematic action designed to produce immediate results.

That word systematic is the key. A culture of urgency requires constant attention to the system itself, every part of it. Any part likely to block or delay progress needs to be identified and fixed in every area. Every part is either adding value to the whole or should be eliminated or replaced with something that is. Any and every problem needs not just to be fixed but also examined for any underlying systemic flaws that need deeper attention.

This might sound like nothing more than elementary supply chain management but goes further to include things like organizational design, business strategy, corporate policy, executive decision making, financial delegations and administrative support systems. A disaster demands attention to all these. It is an opportunity for leaders to streamline every aspect of business, particularly in distant head offices and administrative back rooms where small delays can lead to much longer ones for those at the sharp end in the field.

Disaster leadership, therefore, is not something to be left solely to those in the field. It should start with those in head office who need to invert their organizational modalities to support field operations instead of merely sitting over them. Preferably, head office should report to the field commander instead of the other way around, impractical wishful thinking though this is but a point to consider nonetheless. Issues that any one individual cannot solve within a given time need to be escalated up the chain of command with ever-shrinking deadlines imposed on each higher level in the hierarchy until dealt with—and with immediacy.

It is this that ultimately counts, the immediacy of pushing things through *now* rather than *later*. Perfection in this regard is less important than speed. Near enough is often good enough within reason. An imperfect now is better than a perfect later. Those taking the associated risks should be rewarded, not punished. Lessons should be constantly learned and implemented, not left to be recorded in some later report.

That is the business of disaster leadership.

CHAPTER FIVE

Questions to Ask

Leadership involves more thinking (and organizing) than doing. Thinking is prompted by questions. Leaders ask lots. They ask them of themselves and others.

The questions need not be terribly clever. They can be as simple as: *what do I do next?* None of the answers may be immediately clear or palatable. That matters less than the attempt to find them. A questioning mind is, in general, a thinking one.

Since disasters leave little time for thinking, however, I thought the following list of pre-prepared questions might be helpful. They don't cover all issues, just the common ones I've had to deal with in making my own contributions to disaster recovery.

I've grouped them into four areas: the operating environment, planning, technical requirements and teamwork. Disaster leaders need to grapple with all four.

Operating Environment

Physical Conditions

- What is the geography? How isolated is it?
- What maps or pictures are available?
- What is the climate like now and how might it change? How should we prepare for this?
- What are the physical risks from fire, flood, landslides and the like? How can we guard against these or at least limit their potential impact on our people and the affected communities?

Living Conditions

- How will we live on location? What accommodation services are there? What condition are they in?
- How will our food be provided, stored and prepared?
- What water and sanitation facilities are available?
- Will we need to provide all or any extra facilities of our own? Where will we base these? How will we provision them?

Logistics

- How will we get around? Do we need local guides and drivers?
- What supplies do we need? Where will be get them?
- What is the supply chain? Where is it weakest or broken? How can it be repaired? What are the workarounds?
- What logistical facilities and services must we provide ourselves? What can we borrow from or share with others?

Communication
- How will we communicate among ourselves and with our support crews and head office outside the disaster area?
- What communication infrastructure exists? How reliable is it? What do we do if it breaks down, particularly in an emergency?
- What equipment must we provide ourselves? How will we maintain this?

Emergency Facilities
- What will we do if anyone is injured or gets sick? How will we evacuate or be treated?
- How close are the nearest health facilities? What standard are they? How will we get to them?
- What if the problems are serious, possibly life threatening?
- What skills and capacities do we need to be self-sufficient in case of an injury or illness?

Social Conditions
- What are the defining qualities of the local community?
- What language(s) does it speak?
- What is the predominant religion?
- What are the cultural norms and expectations? What are the taboos?
- Is the community stable or fractious? Who are its leaders?
- What are the potential flash points?
- Who controls the resources?

- Who are the most vulnerable? How are women and children treated? How can we protect the vulnerable from predators?
- How will we communicate with the community and its leaders? Do we need translators? What are their required attributes?

Security

- Where might we be vulnerable from physical attack or extortion? What form might it take?
- What authorities are responsible for protecting us? Are they reliable? How can we work productively with them?
- If their services are questionable, how do we protect ourselves from harm? How can we limit its potential?
- How do we prevent our own hysteria from becoming a self-reinforcing threat?
- Can we engage locals to watch over us? What is required to do this? Can we give jobs to the local community to give them an interest in looking after us? Should we appoint some as security guards?

Corruption and Connivance

- Who must we work with to deliver our services? How competent, clean or corrupt are they?
- How will they conspire to get resources from us? In what way might they block or undermine us?
- How do we fight these practices? What are the trade-offs if we fail? What moral compromises must we accept as the price of delivering humanitarian aid?

Political Considerations

- Who has what political authority in our area of operations—local and national? What role do they play in the disaster response? What is the administrative architecture through which they operate? What is their agenda?
- What formal and informal authorities do they have? What support can we offer them?
- What authorities and approvals do we need from them? What is the best way to secure these?
- How do we engage with officials generally? How do we link and coordinate with their programs and activities?
- What reporting requirements do they have? How can we meet these in the simplest, most cost-effective way?

Planning

Assumptions

- What do we think we are doing? Why are we doing it? What do we assume in doing it? How valid are our assumptions?
- What scenarios are likely to test our assumptions? What should we do if any or all prove invalid? Should we stop, review and change course or just carry on regardless perhaps with some slight modifications?
- Can we avoid over committing before we have a better idea about what we are getting ourselves into?
- What do our stakeholders expect? Is this reasonable? How can we align these expectations with reality?

Strategy

- What are our objectives? How will we go about achieving them?
- Where will we focus our energies? What outcome do we want in each area? What outputs will deliver this?
- How will we know if we are succeeding or failing?
- What might go wrong? How will we respond if it does?

Organizing

- What is the best structure to do what we want?
- Who reports to who and on what basis? What delegations are required?
- Who will do what, when, where and how?
- How will issues be flagged and escalated? Who will do what, how and when in response?

Business Focus

- What particular area of disaster response and recovery are we most suited for and can make the greatest contribution in? Is it possible to limit ourselves to this or can we also contribute in wider areas without weakening our core expertise?
- What are our transferable competencies and capacities? How can we minimize bracket creep should we step beyond our areas of core competence?
- Can we fund others to do the required work instead of doing it ourselves?

Supply Model

- Should we bring all the components in and assemble them ourselves as and when we need them, outsource a turnkey solution or have a mix-and-match approach?

- If we develop a turnkey solution, who is the best supplier?
- How can we ensure the supplier's product can adapt to different circumstances and requirements?
- How can we manage the outsourcing and delivery process while still focusing on our core skill areas?

Delivery Model

- What is the best way to deliver our products and services? Should we do it ourselves or work with another organization or through another process?
- If we need to build or repair houses, for instance, should we do this through contractors or an owner/builder approach?
- Can we use the owner/builder approach as a developmental or psychological tool for affected communities?
- What practical training is required? Can we use the process to qualify local trades people?
- Will any resulting delays be politically acceptable? What do we do if they are not?

Location, Re-location and Land

- Where should we base our activities? What are the advantages and disadvantages? Should we consider another location or locations?
- If we are delivering essential food and water supplies, how likely is it that people will congregate where we do this? What are the implications? Should we deliver the supplies in a different way or in different areas to

disperse or reshape where affected communities locate?

- Should we encourage and support affected communities in returning to where they previously lived or encourage relocating them to other areas?

Land Planning

- If relocation is desired or required, how can we undertake the planning as an urgent priority (as many other things will depend on it)?
- Where is the best location? What infrastructure, services and support systems are required? How do we do the site planning?
- How do we prioritize building?
- How do we engage communities in the planning process and subsequent logistics?
- How long will all this take? What will it cost? Is it politically, socially, economically and financially feasible?
- What are the alternatives? Are we better to leave things as they are? What interim arrangements are needed such as transitional housing?

Process

- How do we manage our entry into a new disaster?
- How do we position our program to help in the best possible way?
- How do we manage the inevitable exhaustion of our people over the course of delivering our program?
- How do we protect ourselves against the dangers of despair or victory disease?

- How do we exit with grace and dignity while endeavoring the leave things better than the way we found them?
- How do we embed the genuine lessons we learn into organizational policies, business systems, operational practices and cultural behaviours?

Technical Requirements

Information

- What information do we need to deliver our emergency services?
- Are there maps of the area? Who has the best ones? How do we get a copy?
- Who is our target community? How many people are involved? What are they likely to need? How and when can we confirm this? Can we simply assume the need and begin delivery?
- How do we keep track of who we have helped, what services we have provided, where the gaps are and what else we need to do?
- What information systems do we need? How will we keep them up to date? What strategic insights do we want them to give us?
- How do we minimize overlaps and redundancies?

Technical Skills and Capacities

- What skill sets do we need to work effectively? Where will we get them? How much will they cost? What will we do if they are not available or we can't afford them? What technical leadership will they need to get the best results?

- How should they be organized and deployed? For what duration?
- What policy frameworks do we need before engaging them? How will we accommodate any policy changes their engagement will require?

Reporting

- What reports are required to meet our obligations to sponsors and superiors? How do we ensure their preparation does not distract or detract from core operations?
- What are the minimum reporting requirements? How do we avoid duplication?
- Are there better reporting systems and formats? Can we report by video or phone rather than in writing? Can we use social media?
- If we must report in writing, can it be by exception rather than occurrence?

Waving the Flag

- How do we promote our activities to donors and sponsors?
- What products will best illustrate what we are doing and how well we are doing it?
- How do we frame and communicate our challenges?
- How do we ensure that any promotional activities do not distort or misrepresent our contributions?

Strategic Capacities

- What minimum overarching capacities must we have in place to succeed?

- What resources do we need to stay in touch with and be relevant to the main players?
- What strategic outreach capacities (for advocating, lobbying, representing and so on) do we need to connect with other contributors without being run over by them?
- What over-the-horizon predictive tools and capacities should we have in place to identify, prepare for or mitigate potential problems that could bring us unstuck?
- How do we cope with surge demands that might otherwise threaten to overload us?

Coordination

- What other groups and organizations are providing disaster response and recovery services in our area of operation?
- What coordination clusters work? Which ones are a waste of time? Are any politically dangerous and, if so, how?
- Where do our interests and values align? Where do they diverge?
- How do we link and coordinate with productive partners? What value does each of us bring to our mutual contributions? How do we leverage these contribution?
- Is there a better way to engage with each other? Where are the gaps and overlaps?
- How should we meet and communicate? With what regularity? How do we decide? What do we share?

Delivery Philosophy

- Does our approach encourage strong community engagement that slows reconstruction or does it support fast-track construction that risks community exclusion for a quicker result?
- Does it involve getting communities to build their own houses to create greater involvement and ownership or does it deliver houses through contractors?
- Does it promote a process of constant review and improvement whereby best practices are constantly learnt and transferred across an entire recovery program or merely to individual constructions?

Communication

- Who do we need to communicate with? What do we want and need to communicate?
- How should we position ourselves? What are the issues?
- What messages do we want to convey? Who is best placed to convey them? What are the best vehicles to use?

Social Media

- How can we use this without our time being eaten up or wasted by it? What will give us the biggest possible impact? Do we need a dedicated social communicator?
- Can regular tweets or Facebook posts substitute for more formal reports?

- What approvals are needed for public comment by individual team members, what disclaimers?
- What is reasonable to communicate on social media, what is not?
- How do we keep on top of what anyone publishes? Do we need to?
- Where could we get ourselves into trouble with social media? What will we do if a problem occurs?

Celebrity Visits
- How do we take advantage of any potential celebrity or VIP visits while minimizing their distortions?
- How can we ensure the ignorance of any views visitors express do not damage our programs and services?

The Team

Forming a Team
- What sort of team do we need to manage our overall contribution?
- How should it be organized? Who should do what? What is a fair division of labor?
- Do the individual roles and responsibilities feel meaningful to those assigned them? How and when should they be reviewed?

Leading a Team
- What tone should the leader adopt—determined, serious, friendly, understanding, supportive?
- What leadership style is appropriate—directive, facilitative, *lazier faire*, egalitarian? In what circumstances?

- What decisions should the leader, team as a whole and individual members make?
- What shared values should we create and appeal to in shaping the team culture?

Engaging a Team

- How should team members be brought together and introduced, particularly new ones?
- In forming the team, how can the potential ructions of storming be minimized or avoided?
- What normative outcomes can be engineered?
- How can contributing to the team itself become one of the highest values collectively aspired to?

Managing a Team

- Which team processes need formal management? Which ones do not?
- How often should a team meet formally? In what way? For what reason?
- How should these meetings be conducted? How can we tell if they are working as well as they should? What can we do if they are not?
- What conversations should be left to individuals to conduct among themselves? When and on what basis should these individuals advise their colleagues about what they have discussed or decided?

Managing Individual Performance

- What individual characteristics or behaviours could bring the team unstuck?
- What are the most practical indicators of success and failure?

- What interventions are required to prevent or minimize disruptions?
- At what point and on what basis should individual team members be invited to leave for the benefit of the team as a whole?

Contributing to a Team

- What does each member of the team want or need from his or her colleagues to work effectively? What does each member expect?
- How can roles be integrated most effectively to minimize friction? How can gaps and overlaps be sorted?
- How can a culture of open, professional collegiality be forged among the members?

Maintaining a Team

- Appreciating that responding to disasters is enormously demanding on those involved, what can we do to ease or release any built up pressures within the team?
- What common activities can we share? How can we celebrate success together? What ethos can we develop to quickly bounce back from setbacks?

Refreshing a Team

- When and how can we bring in new blood to refresh the team? What new skills might we need at what stages of recovery operations? How do we determine and agree on this?
- How do we select new people and bring them up to speed as quickly and effectively as we can? What

problems might we experience with the new dynamics? How should other team members adapt?

CHAPTER SIX

Rising to the Occasion

Leadership is not easy. Indeed, it is one of the most difficult of all disciplines.

It is not a popularity contest. As a leader you will be called on to make many hard decisions. Among them will be that those that merely disappoint and those so unpopular they make you enemies. This is regrettable but a fact of life.

The worst thing you can do is try to please everyone. If you do, you are likely to please no one. People will see you as a weak and vacillating. While they might smile at you and tell you are wonderful, deep down you will lose the most important interpersonal enabler of all—their respect.

Nicolai Machiavelli wrote in *The Prince* that it is safer to be respected than loved. This is true for all leaders. But it does not mean you need make others fear you. Fear breeds resentment, hatred even, not respect. That is not the way to go.

Leadership is ultimately a balancing act. It requires judgment, common sense, a common touch. Leaders need to show restraint along with enthusiasm, caution along with bold initiative, warmth and sensitivity along with a steely resolve, engagement along with detachment.

Getting the balance right is not easy. Indeed, it is all but impossible, certainly in all matters in all things for all people. Don't fret over this. Making mistakes comes with the leadership territory. It is not making them that matters so much as what you do about them when you do.

Those who are insensitive to or ignore their mistakes, weaknesses and failings are a danger to themselves and others. Those who genuinely note, acknowledge and learn from them, adapting their approach accordingly, are generally not. Those willing to go a step further by apologizing to those their errors upset or harm are likely to win not just the respect of followers but their loyalty and ongoing commitment too.

Heartfelt apologies together with heartfelt acknowledgement and thanks for the constructive contributions go a long way in establishing the respect, trust and warmth that are the good oil of all human relationships. Leaders need to offer them charitably, although without going over the top. Too much is soppy and will merely devalue what a leader says. Too little creates emotional gaps where others wonder why they bother contributing at all.

Again, balance is required. And judgment. These two fundamental qualities are essential to being effective as a leader no matter how elusive they may be from time to time.

In the end, it is often the smallest things that make the biggest difference, like saying please and thank you. People need to feel welcome and acknowledged for their contributions. They need to feel respected too. And protected. And secure. They need to feel that they and what they do are valuable and valued. They need to feel that they are making a real contribution through a meaningful role that constructively connects with and adds to the wider team and its higher aspirations.

Leaders who ignore, trash or trample on these feelings will in short order turn constructive contributions into destructive political games. So will any power vacuum they create by their failure to intervene when any individual team member sours.

Discerning which problems are caused by a failure of leadership and which are caused by flaws of individual character within the team are, again, far from easy, just essential. Leaders must nip problems in the bud, be they self-induced or created by others. Dealing with problems and problem people, including themselves, is not just part of the job, it is often *the* most important part.

But problems are just that—problems. They will always exist, particularly in a crisis environment. Leaders will be judged both by those they cause and those they prevent and resolve. Good leaders will understand and appreciate this. Great leaders will relish it, for a joy in problem-solving lies at the enabling heart of leadership. A person who runs from problems is no leader at all while one who embraces them with delight in search of a constructive solution most certainly is.

Of course, leadership goes well beyond just seeking, finding and solving problems. Leaders do this as part of a journey toward a particular destination. Call it what you want: a vision, goal, purpose, aspiration, end point, outcome, impact or whatever. It is the reason *why* we do things. Leaders need to be no less clear on this as on the *what* and *how*. All three are important.

While the *what* and *how* may be far less clear in the early stages of a disaster, good leaders must determine a course of action regardless. They must craft order from chaos by bringing a semblance of organization to the recovery process no matter how muddy the situation may at first be or appear. It is what leaders do regardless of whether their early decisions are right or wrong. Adjusting and correcting as things become clearer is part of the job.

This is the business of leadership, disaster leadership in particular. It is a business that forges character no less than revealing it. Good leaders rise to the occasion. I hope you are one who does and that this little handbook helps you do so.

Appreciation

Thank you for taking the time to read *Building Back from Disaster*. I hope you found it of interest. Feel free to let me know either way. You can email me at bill@nicolnotes.com or find more on what I have written at www.nicolnotes.com. As an independent, self-funded author, I appreciate and rely on the support of readers like yourself to help me continue researching and writing books like this. You'll find pointers to others I have written on the same subject in the following pages. I hope to publish more and will also gradually make my pre-digital backlist available on the internet.

Tsunami Chronicles

Adventures in Disaster Management

Few natural disasters come bigger than the 2004 tsunami. It left a trail of destruction from one side of the Indian Ocean to the other. Hardest hit was Aceh in Indonesia's west where the tsunami killed almost a quarter of a million people and left half million homeless as it smashed into a strip of coastline 800 kilometers long and several kilometers wide. The global community rallied to help in the largest military deployment since World War II. It then spent billions rebuilding Aceh in one of the most challenging reconstruction programs of its kind. *Tsunami Chronicles: Adventures in Disaster Management* tells the inside story of recovery. Written by the Indonesian Government's senior advisor for tsunami recovery, Bill Nicol, it lays bare the tectonic political and managerial forces that swept along the rebuilding program with no less force than the tsunami itself. This is a powerful, first-hand narrative from a highly experienced journalist, author and consultant who played a pivotal role in the recovery operations. A series of six books in one book, *Tsunami Chronicles* offers rare and unique insights that will annoy some, anger a few, excite others and inspire many. It will appeal to anyone with an interest in international development and disaster recovery—humanitarian volunteers, aid workers, consultants, engineers, agency staff, institutional managers, policy makers and political leaders—as well as academics, students of management, business leaders and the general public.

Print copies available from Amazon Create Space
https://www.createspace.com/4226145

The complete Kindle Edition is available from
http://www.amazon.com/dp/B00Q084VVU

Each of the six individual books in the series
are also separately available through ebook distributors

Tsunami

A Poet's Journey

Earthquakes and tsunamis are two of humanity's greatest natural threats. The mightier they are the more deadly they are, and few were more deadly than the earthquake that ripped open the floor of the Indian Ocean on Boxing Day 2004 unleashing massive waves of death and destruction to steal the lives of a quarter million people from 50 countries. Then the world's greatest natural disaster, certainly its most widespread in terms of human impact, the Boxing Day Tsunami hit Indonesia's western-most province, Aceh, hardest. Aceh was tsunami central. Rebuilding it and the lives of its shattered community is one of the great recovery stories of human history. Yet, ten years later, the achievement is barely remembered except by a few closely involved. One is author and poet Bill Nicol who played a central role in rebuilding Aceh in four short years. Working at the blistering coalface of recovery as a deeply committed humanitarian, he shored up success while fighting and defeating the deep corruption, incompetence and political obstruction that daily threatened the multi-billion-dollar recovery effort. *Tsunami: A Poet's Journey* captures the hot belly of passion and politics that drove and ripped at the fabric of Aceh's tsunami recovery. It's a poet's gift of remembrance for the 10th anniversary that adds to his earlier investigations in *Tsunami Chronicles* and *Crisis Leadership*.

Print edition available from Amazon Create Space
https://www.createspace.com/5103913

Amazon Kindle ebook available from
http://www.amazon.com/dp/B00PW9GJ3Q

Crisis Leadership

Dealing with Disasters from Asia to Africa and America

Terrorism. Tsunamis. Earthquakes. Epidemics. What do they have in common? Each is a crisis. Each requires an urgent response. Each demands leadership—crisis leadership—to recover and rebound. But what is crisis leadership? When does it succeed? What makes it fail? Crisis Leadership answers these questions by drawing on examples including the 9/11 terrorist attack on New York, the author's tsunami experience, Japan's tsunami, Typhoon Haiyan in the Philippines, Haiti's earthquake, genocide in Sudan and the latest Ebola outbreak in West Africa that is now threatening the world. This timely and controversial work will appeal to anyone keen to understand the many crisis we face, what we can learn from them and how we can respond in creating a better, safer world.

Print edition available from Amazon Create Space
https://www.createspace.com/5103913

Amazon Kindle ebooks available from
http://www.amazon.com/dp/B00PFO1GLS

www.ingramcontent.com/pod-product-compliance
Lightning Source LLC
Chambersburg PA
CBHW070257290326
41930CB00041B/2631